TAKING PART

A Caring School

by Sally Hewitt

Photographs by Chris Fairclough

This edition 2006

Franklin Watts
338 Euston Road
London NW1 3BH

Franklin Watts Australia
Hachette Children's Books
Level 17/207 Kent St, Sydney, NSW 2000

Copyright © 2002 Franklin Watts

ISBN: 0 7496 6659 5
Dewey Decimal Classification: 371.4'047
A CIP catalogue reference for this book is available from the British
Library.

Printed in Malaysia

Editor: Kate Banham
Designer: Joelle Wheelwright
Art Direction: Peter Scoulding
Photography: Chris Fairclough

Acknowledgements
The publishers would like to thank the staff and pupils of Latchmere
Junior School, Kingston-on-Thames, Surrey, for their help in the
production of this book. The photographs on page 9 were kindly
supplied by Latchmere Junior School.

Contents

(Words printed in **_bold italics_** are explained in the glossary.)

The Whole School

 Children, staff and parents at Latchmere Junior School all get involved in making sure their school is a stimulating, safe and happy place to be. The pupils helped to write the school code and they take *responsibility* for keeping it – in the classrooms, in the playground and everywhere in the school.

Parents, teachers and children discuss things together.

We, the children, teachers, support staff and parents, aim to make our school a happy and safe place, by following this code of behaviour.

Code of behaviour

The school code is not just a list pinned to a notice board. It is a way of behaving that everyone knows about and tries to follow wherever they are and whatever they are doing at school.

Point 1 of the code: 'We will be polite, considerate and helpful towards others at all times.'

Point 2 of the code: 'We will respect and care for ourselves, other people and their belongings, the school and the school property.'

Visitors to the school find the children doing their best to keep to the last point of the code.

We will behave in a quiet and sensible manner in all parts of the school.

Point 3 of the code: 'We will walk along corridors and verandahs and be safety conscious at all times.'

Questions

Why do you think it's a good idea for the pupils to help write the school code?

What point would you like to include in your school code?

Point 4 of the code: 'At playtimes, we will be kind and considerate towards others and not play roughly.'

It's Up To Me!

 There are only a few school *rules* so they are easy to remember. Everyone knows what will happen if they choose to keep – or to break – them. They know that the way they behave is up to them!

The children agree that the school rules are important.

When you've done something wrong you think – why did I do this? I'm going to stop it now!

If I'm chatting and someone else is trying to read, I'm spoiling it for them.

Achievement Award

Presented to:
Georgia Mills
On the 19th of July 2001

In recognition of the consistent effort you maintained over the year with your role of 'Road Safety Officer'. It has been a delight to see you take this role so seriously and the whole school have benefited from your creativity and initiatives. Well done.

Signed

Praise

Being **encouraged** and praised makes everyone feel good and want to try hard in everything they do. Hard work and good behaviour is rewarded in Achievement Assemblies and with stickers, stamps and certificates.

Team points

Everyone belongs to one of the four school teams – Lions, Tigers, Leopards or Jaguars. Each team is a mixture of all ages. Brothers and sisters are usually in the same team. Children try hard to win points not just for themselves, but for their teams.

All the events on Sports Day are team events. Every point won goes to the team.

The team with the most points wins the team cup.

9

In the Classroom

 At the start of the autumn term, each class discusses what their classroom code of behaviour will be for the year ahead. When they have all agreed, the code is pinned up on the notice board where everyone can see it.

↑ The children remind themselves of their classroom code.

Classroom Code

• Do not speak while others are speaking.
• Try your hardest all of the time.
• Listen carefully to instructions.
• Put your hand up when you want to talk. Do not call out.
• Be kind, helpful and have respect for others.
• Keep the room tidy and return things when you have used them.

Tidiness Cup

Each year, the school awards a cup to the class that keeps their room tidiest throughout the year. When 4B was flooded and the floor had to be taken up, the children thought they wouldn't stand a chance of winning the tidiness cup. They were surprised and delighted when they won it for keeping their classroom tidy under very difficult conditions.

Happy and hardworking

Although every classroom code is different, they all encourage kindness, consideration, hard work and tidiness. The children understand how important it is to keep to their code because they helped to make it up themselves.

Listening carefully helps everyone to learn and follow instructions. ↑

It's easier to do your best when everyone around you is trying their hardest too. ↓

Putting your hand up and listening to others means that everyone has a chance to be heard. ↑

Questions

Why do you think keeping the classroom tidy is important?

What rules can you think of that help to make everyone in the classroom happy?

Circle Time

Each class has a Circle Time, where children take part in activities and games that help them to feel strong and confident. If you're feeling worried or unsure of yourself, it's harder to make friends and to do your best at school.

↑ The whole class sit in a circle and listen to instructions from their teacher.

↑ Could this feeling be amazement?

Silent feelings

Sometimes you can tell what a person is feeling just by how they are holding their body and the look on their face. The children take it in turns to act out a **feeling** – without saying a word.

Birthday order

One of the games the children play during Circle Time is the Birthday Game. The children are given the task of organising themselves around the circle in order of their birthdays. One child says their birthday – e.g. 20th April – then the rest have to find where to sit by asking questions and changing places. When everyone eventually settles down again the children go around the circle calling out their birthdays. It's amazing – everyone is sitting in the right place!

What a muddle! We'll never sort this out!

This isn't taking as long as I thought it would.

My birthday comes between yours and yours.

Co-operation

The Birthday Game helps the children learn to co-operate with each other. Co-operating means listening to each other's ideas, being helpful and working well together.

13

The Playground

At playtime, the whole school uses the playground. Not everyone wants to be doing the same thing so there are separate areas designed for different kinds of activities.

Some children skip together while others play on the climbing frames. →

Special areas

Whether you want to practise netball, play football, swing, balance or climb, skip, read, chat or play imaginative games – there will be somewhere special for you to do what you choose.

I like the enchanted wood because you can play adventure games and hunt things.

← **The enchanted wood has shady corners and hiding places. It's a good place to use your imagination.**

⬆ You can sit and read, chat with your friends or just think quietly in the quiet area.

⬅ The children helped to design and make the giant leaf sculptures which have turned a dull corner into an interesting place to play.

I like the football area. I play football every day.

You can climb on the sculptures and balance on the logs.

The football area is always busy. Instead of a real football, the players kick around a small, soft ball which can't hurt anyone. ↗

Happy Playtimes

Playtime can be miserable if other children are rough or unkind and you haven't got a friend to play with. A friendly grown-up, the playground code and the *Friendship* Squad all help to make playtime a happy time for everyone.

Playground code

1 Be fair, friendly and kind to others and let them share in your play.
2 Respect other people, their property, apparatus and the garden.
3 Leave the quiet area for those who want to be quiet.
4 Decide the rules of the game before you start to play.
5 Stay in the playground at playtime.
6 Talk through **problems** and try to stay calm. Swearing and bad language are never acceptable.
7 Do as teachers, lunchtime supervisors or monitors ask cheerfully.
8 Keep the playground tidy.
9 Play ball games only in the ball park area of the playground.
10 Leave animal and plant life unharmed.
11 Avoid rough games.
12 Treat others as you would like to be treated yourself.

Playground code

Like all the school codes, the children helped to put together the playground code. They know that keeping it helps to make sure they have a good time – and that everyone else does too!

Mrs Johnson is the social skills assistant. The children look for her if they need any help.

The Friendship Squad

Children of any age can apply to belong to the Friendship Squad. Once they have joined, Mrs Johnson teaches them how to do their new job. One of their responsibilities is to keep a look-out at playtime for anyone who is **lonely** or unhappy. If they see someone in trouble, they know what to do.

↑ The Friendship Squad enjoy their work.

Some children who join the Friendship Squad know what it's like to be lonely at playtime. ↑

If you see someone looking sad, you go and help them.

Questions

Why do you think a Friendship Squad is a good idea?

What could you do to help someone who is lonely at playtime?

I joined because I'd been getting a bit lonely and I knew how upsetting it could be.

The Friendship Bench

Anyone who has lost their friends or is feeling lonely and left out at playtime can go and sit on the Friendship Bench. A member of the Friendship Squad will see them sitting there and go over to help.

↑
The smiling faces on the sign remind the children that they can be smiling too.

Smiling faces

If you want to find the Friendship Bench, you can't miss it! The big colourful sign makes certain it's the first thing you see when you walk into the playground.

← **It's no fun feeling lonely.**

Don't be lonely!

There's no need to be lonely for very long. If you sit on the Friendship Bench someone will come and play with you, look for your friends or find out if you have a problem and help to solve it.

Sometimes it's hard to find a friend or Mrs Johnson because it's such a big playground – that's when you need the Friendship Bench.

To the rescue

Everyone tries to be friendly and helpful all the time, but sometimes no one notices you're feeling sad and lonely. It's good to have a place to go where you know someone will soon come to the rescue.

There are three children on the Friendship Bench. They don't feel like talking to each other.

Mrs Johnson is there to help solve difficult problems.

Members of the Friendship Squad come along and ask, 'What's wrong? Can I help?'

Questions

What kind of problems do you think the Friendship Squad could solve?

What kind of problems might need help from an adult?

19

Buddies

Latchmere Infant School is in a separate building next to the Junior School. At the end of the summer term, children from year 5 take the children who are coming up from the Infant School on a tour so that they get to know where everything is.

Every new pupil is paired up with a pupil from year 5 who becomes their buddy for the next school year.

Buddies often play together all year round.

Playing together

On the first visit, the buddies spend a playtime together. The older children are responsible for getting to know the younger ones, becoming friends and making sure they have a happy time. When they start school in September, children in year 3 know they have buddies in year 6 they can turn to.

Friends

It's not just the younger children who benefit from having a buddy. The older children enjoy getting to know the younger ones and learn a lot from their new responsibility. Sometimes the buddies get to know each other so well they become really good friends.

Buddies become good friends even though they are different ages.

Growing Up

Buddies enjoy their friendship for a year but then year 6 pupils leave and go to their new schools. By the time year 3 become year 4 they have the confidence to manage without their buddies. Their buddies have helped them to become independent and to start to look out for the new young children coming to school.

We got to know each other, learned all about ourselves. That's how we became friends.

My buddy never lets me down.

Year 3s don't feel nervous or scared because they're friends with their buddies.

Question

If you were a buddy, what would you do to help a new pupil feel at home?

21

Reading Together

Once a week, the buddies read together. The older children help the younger ones but first they get some tips from their teacher. They learn to be patient and encouraging and not to take over the reading themselves.

When they get stuck with a word you've got to give them a chance. If they're really struggling, you can help them.

Reading together is not as easy as it sounds. You have to learn how to do it well.

The children choose a book that they both enjoy.

Choosing a book

First the buddies choose a book together from the library. The older children remember the books they used to enjoy and they make some suggestions. They like to get the chance to re-read some of their old favourites. When the buddies have made their choice, they find somewhere quiet and comfortable to read.

Working it out

Because the buddies read together every week, they soon start to feel confident and relaxed. If the younger one isn't sure of a word, there's no need to feel embarrassed. Their buddy will help them and they can work it out together.

The buddies take time to enjoy the pictures.

It feels good to help someone to get better at something.

Story time

Enjoying books is an important part of reading together so if there's time after all their hard work, the younger children hope that it's their turn to be read to.

When I can't read the words my buddy helps me work it out.

Having a buddy improved my reading.

It's time to settle down and listen to a good story.

23

Mediators

At Latchmere, when friends fall out or an argument develops, the children turn to each other for help. Trained pupil *mediators* act as friends to the children on both sides of the argument and help them sort out their problems.

Mediators always work in pairs.

Training

All year 5 children are asked if they would like to apply for jobs as mediators. Those who get the job are trained during the summer term so they are ready to become mediators in year 6.

Acting out problems

The aim is to help the children work their own way through their disputes and difficulties. Mrs Johnson works with the mediators as they act out problems and learn ways of dealing with them.

The mediators are given a special training course before they can take on the job.

Introducing ourselves!

At the beginning of the school year, the new mediators take an assembly. They introduce themselves and remind the school that they are there to help.

← Two of the girls made up a rap to put over their message.

On duty

The mediators are on duty for a week at a time. Some weeks they might be very busy but at other times they might have no work at all. They wear a Latchmere Junior School Mediator badge so that when a problem develops they can be spotted easily.

Rap

When you've got a problem
Come to us
We'll be a very good friend
And we won't make a fuss

We'll ask you four questions
Fair and square
Don't be shy to answer
We don't care

We'll give you some suggestions
For your **solutions**
Keep it all calm
No revolutions

Then your problems
Should be solved
Remember - if there's an argument
Don't get involved
It can be resolved

When you come to the mediators!

Solving Problems

When children turn to the mediators for help they are taken to a quiet place indoors where they sit together around a table. Before the mediation can start there are a few rules to follow.

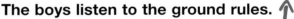 The boys listen to the ground rules.

Ground rules

The children have to sign an agreement to keep the mediation ground rules - if they don't agree, the mediation cannot continue.

The children agree to:
- Speak one at a time.
- Listen carefully to others.
- Speak truthfully.
- Keep hands, feet and objects to themselves.
- Keep calm.

The mediators agree to:
- Be fair.
- Let each other speak in turn.
- Listen without taking sides.
- Remind everyone of the rules if necessary.

Problem solved!

It's not until all this has been done that the mediators find out what the problem is and how the children feel. They talk it through and agree what to do next.

It's smiles all round when a solution has been agreed.

Now these boys are friends again.

Record book

Then the mediators write up a report about the mediation and what was agreed at the end of it. The date and time of the mediation and the names of the children involved are entered in a record book.

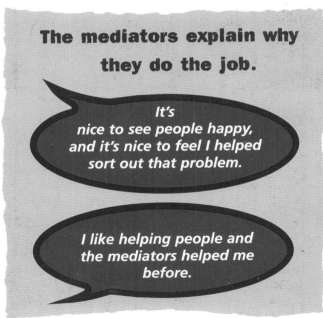

The mediators explain why they do the job.

It's nice to see people happy, and it's nice to feel I helped sort out that problem.

I like helping people and the mediators helped me before.

Glossary

Behaviour

Our behaviour is the way we act, especially towards each other. We can choose to behave well or badly.

Code of behaviour

A code of behaviour is a list of ideas that have been agreed on by everyone involved about the best way to behave in the playground, throughout the school and in the classroom.

Encourage

To encourage someone is to give them hope and strength for something they are trying to do. You might tell them they are doing well or offer some help.

Feelings

Your feelings are the way you respond to how people behave towards you. You can hurt someone's feelings by being unkind to them or make them feel good by being friendly.

Friendship

Friendship is acting in a friendly, caring and helpful way towards your friends day after day. It's not just saying you are a friend, but actually behaving as a friend.

Lonely

Sometimes it feels all right to be alone. Being lonely is feeling sad because you are alone and wishing you had a friend.

Mediator

When two people or two groups of people have an argument or a problem, a mediator is someone who helps them to sort out their problem and become friends again.

Problem

A problem is a difficulty that needs to be sorted out. Two people can have a problem that stops them from being friends.

Responsibility

If you have a responsibility for something, you are in charge. You might be responsible for making sure lights are not left on or for getting your library books back in time.

Rule

A rule is an order that should be obeyed. A school rule could be 'no running in the corridors'. A playground rule could be 'only three children on the climbing frame at a time'.

Solution

A solution is a way of sorting out a problem. The solution to an argument could be that both sides agree to share.

Taking Part

Be a buddy

Older pupils at Latchmere School are special buddies to the new young children. Their friendship lasts all year, and sometimes even longer.

With your class, talk about how having a buddy could have helped you when you first came to school. If you don't have a buddy system, maybe you could set one up.

Solve problems fairly

Mediators at Latchmere School learn how to help solve other children's problems and arguments fairly.

Acting out arguments and problems in class can help you to see how to solve them. If you get into an argument with a friend, ask someone else to help you to sort it out fairly.

Help out

Buddies, mediators and the Friendship Squad at Latchmere School all help to make the school a happy place for everyone.

There are always ways you can be helpful. Helping and being kind to someone else makes them feel good and it makes you feel good too.

Improve your playground

Latchmere playground is divided into areas with interesting things to do. It has football and netball areas, sculptures and climbing frames.

Invite an artist to help you make a playground sculpture or paint a mural. Find out if an organisation will help you to plant a garden or build a climbing frame.

Index